I Don't Do Updates

...BUT YOU SHOULD

By Circe Denyer

Copyright © 2016 Circe Denyer

ISBN: 978-1540415349
ISBN-10:1540415341

DEDICATION

To the clients and friends that have asked me to update their computer while I was doing the routine maintenance. It was the questions you asked that prompted me to write this book.

DISCLAIMER

This book is not intended to give you advice. Nor is it
a guarantee you will not have problems when you
update your computer. It is to provide insight as to
what can happen to your computer if you do not do
updates, and why they are an important part of
computer maintenance.

CONTENTS

ACKNOWLEDGMENTS

Linnaea Mallette, my friend and business partner in many adventures. She helped me to be motivated to .produce this work and the others that will follow in the series I am calling "I Don't". Her sincere encouragement was perfect to get me started.

"An update is available for your computer"

1. I DON'T UPDATE

I hear this all of the time.

Computers have an uncanny ability, without saying a word, to intimidate their owner. It is as if they are a live entity; something that a person could kill.

People can kill computers, but it takes doing things over time and not paying attention to the basic things that keep a computer healthy. It is the same as your own health.

You can kill your computer by NOT doing routine, regular updates. In this book, I am going to walk you through the updates process and the updates that every computer owner should do to optimize your computer's health.

2. WHY SHOULD I UPDATE?

Computers require updates to keep them running without "crashing". Crashing is a term computer people use to describe a computer that has stopped working. It may be showing a screen in blue and white (PC) or paper white (MAC) with a message (usually cryptic) that indicates something went wrong. On a PC, before version 10 of Windows®, the screen has very technical wording. Most people do not understand, but know it looks severely broken. It is called the Blue Screen of Death, or BSOD.

It is not really dead. It is mostly dead.

> "There's a big difference between mostly dead and all dead. Mostly dead is slightly alive."- Miracle Max, *"The Princess Bride"*

Computers require updates to make the interaction of the programs and the components work better.

There is something called ***vulnerability*** in the computer industry. Viruses, infections and invasion by hackers happen because computers become vulnerable. When a company discovers a vulnerability in its software, an update is issued to remove that vulnerability. Like shutting the door and locking it. Those updates close the door so your computer is not vulnerable to these attacks.

Some programs are more susceptible to hacking than others. Hackers often program their infections on the more susceptible ones. It is not necessary to know which programs are vulnerable. Update the programs and the operating system on your computer. This will prevent more harm in less time than researching prone programs.

Hackers will also develop programs to attack programs that "everybody uses" so that their efforts will cause widespread infection. This is the primary reason that Windows® is more commonly infected than MAC® computers. This will not always be the case.

The components of your computer work better when the updates for these components are current.

Some of the components of a standard computer are the hard drive, the CD/DVD drive, the mouse, the keyboard, the monitor and the sound component.

The updates for these components are called drivers.

"LIKE CAR ACCIDENTS, MOST HARDWARE PROBLEMS ARE DUE TO DRIVER ERROR."

…drivers are necessary in a computer to make things work together smoother.

3. WHAT IS THIS THING CALLED A DRIVER?

Computers contain parts and software from several companies and developers. The label on the box may say Hewlett Packard® or Dell®, but the parts inside the computer come from Microsoft®, Western Digital®, Intel®, Gigabyte®, Micro Star International®, AMD®, NVidia® and more.

The updates in this category are called drivers.

The relationship of these manufactures to one another require that they provide drivers that connect the physical parts with the software you use. They also provide the updates.

You use software programs to surf the web, write email, create artwork or write your next blog post. If the software is not written correctly for the components it is designed to interact with, things go wrong. When a manufacturer discovers a faulty driver, they write an update for it

Drivers are critical to the smooth running of your computer. Drivers are also the more complex of all the updates.

Frequently, drivers are not updated because the system does not have a notification process to alert the computer owner.

Frequently, drivers do not need updating.

See how complicated this part can be?

> "Computers are like Old Testament Gods; Lots of rules and no mercy."
>
> -Joseph Campbell

Updating the driver may solve a problem with a component, but, warnings are in place on most driver updates because a driver update may not be compatible with other parts such as the operating system.

Driver updates are best done in order. Version 1.1 before version 2.1 etc. This is not always required and if you have a computer technician do it, they will normally jump to the latest and only do the older ones if that newest update does not work. Many times the newest update rolls in all the previous updates into the most current one.

I recommend for most computer users to have a technician evaluate the problem before updating the drivers.

The drivers that often are the exception to this recommendation are video drivers (NVidia®, AMD®, and Intel®). The video drivers manage a portion of the computer that controls how it looks on the screen. They help to speed up the startup time and are especially important in video and image processing.

"NEVER ASK WHAT SORT OF
COMPUTER A GUY DRIVES. IF HE'S A
MAC® USER, HE'LL TELL YOU. IF NOT,
WHY EMBARRASS HIM?"

-Tom Clancy

4. I HAVE A MAC

As a Microsoft Windows® user, I still love MAC's too. MAC's have updates. MAC® updates are not automatic, you have to initiate the update.

MAC® updates are called "Software Updates". Everything you need is included for the MAC® to get what it needs to work properly. Simple.

All MAC® users should regularly check and do "Software Updates".

How do you do that?

You should back up your MAC® before you begin.

Tap the Apple icon at the top left of your Mac's main menu bar, and choose "Software Update..."

Follow the instructions on the screen and check the computer to make sure all is well after you are finished.

"WINDOWS® UPDATE KEEPS WINDOWS®, INTERNET EXPLORER, AND MICROSOFT OFFICE UP-TO-DATE WITH THE LATEST SECURITY PATCHES AND BUG FIXES, ENSURING YOUR COMPUTER IS AS SECURE AS POSSIBLE"

5. WINDOWS® UPDATES

This is the most important of all the updates a computer user can do.

Windows® software controls the computer; and all of the programs you add to it function using some part of that Windows® software.

Microsoft uses the term Windows® for many different things. It is the name of the operating system and the name of the screen you see when you start up the computer; the program boxes that contain the game you play or the upgrade window you look at, - these are all "windows."

Updating Windows® means you are updating the operating system. This keeps the system secure and working properly.

When you run the Windows® update you will receive many files, with many names. The simplest statement I can make about this is, let it happen and make note of anything that "fails".

Failed updates happen for a number of reasons.

Often it is because you do not have the component Windows® is trying to update.

The computer may reboot while doing updates. Then when it starts back up, begin another set of updates.

Each update has its own behavior. It may seem complex, but, in most cases, it does what it is designed to do without issue.

Most of the time.

"THE SHORTEST HORROR STORY EVER-
COMPUTER UNABLE TO CONNECT TO
THE INTERNET"

6. SECURITY UPDATES

You bought your computer to surf the web, email friends and family and shop online. Skipping security updates can hinder and eventually stop your computers' ability to connect to the Internet.

Security updates protect the computer from viruses and other forms of computer infections that allow the computer to be controlled from another computer without your knowledge.

A computer may still be connected to the Internet, but cannot browse the web because it will not load a website or send emails. The connection to the Internet, however, remains in place and provides an open door to more infections which cause severe damage.

Security updates are part of the Windows® update component. In the updates section you can choose certain update to be done. I suggest you allow Windows® to choose and that would include security updates.

"I WISH I HAD SPENT MORE TIME
ALONE WITH MY COMPUTER."

-Danielle Bunten Berry

7. WHEN SHOULD I UPDATE?

My short answer is "often." My long answer has to do with your computer lifestyle and habits.

If your computer is left turned on all of the time, you can set updates to be automatic and they will be done in the wee hours of the morning on Windows® computers. If you are in the habit of closing down the computer and turning it off at the end of the day, you should change the updates time and day setting to accommodate your schedule.

Important Note:

> The computer will often reboot after an update. Scheduling your update time assures you will not be surprised by the computer rebooting in the middle of something important, like a presentation.
>
> It is wise to close all programs and documents you have been working on before you walk away from a computer that is set to do automatic updates. A computer reboot will close open programs and restart the system as

if you turned off the switch.

Some programs save a copy of the work and some do not. Why take the chance? Close all your work and then leave the computer.

Updates for all versions except version 10 can be set to:

- Downloaded but not installed until you do it yourself
- Downloaded and installed at a certain time of the day
- Be manually downloaded and installed.

The default setting is automatically receive updates and is set for 3:00 am.

Windows® 10 does not have user settings for these controls. You can tweak it, but it is not obvious. The controls you do have in version 10 allow you to set your normal computer use time and Windows® will do updates but not reboot the computer during that time.

I also recommend, for those of you that leave your computer on all of the time, rebooting once a month by turning the computer completely off and then turning it back on. There are some updates that do not complete the installation unless the computer is restarted from power off.

Non-Windows® updates, such as those for your anti-malware program, should be done as soon as you get notification.

Most free programs require your interaction. They are not done unless you call them up to do them.

Other paid-for software such as Microsoft Office® does not have an automatic setting and you must do it yourself.

In the words of Nike®, "just do it."

"THE TRUTH IS OUT THERE."

-The X Files, TV show

8. UPDATE OR UPGRADE?

Updates are free. Upgrades cost money. Updates are necessary, upgrades are not always necessary.

If you purchased a program for your computer and it notifies you that there is an upgrade, you can investigate the features of the program and decide if this is something you need to continue using it. Some programs require upgrading to be compatible with the newer operating system. In that case, the upgrade would be a necessity.

If you downloaded a program that was listed as free, but you signed up for a free trial to get extra features, when the trial is over, you will have to upgrade to keep those features. If you chose not to upgrade, there is usually a way to continue using it as a free program.

Some shareware programs that are available on the Internet are always free. These can often install other programs during installation of the one you want. These other programs may pop up requesting upgrades. Careful reading of the screens that appear during updates will prevent accidental installation of programs you did not want.

At the end of this book, I will list some of my favorite programs and the cautions of installing them.

All programs except those that are no longer being supported will require an update at some point and your program will notify you via a pop-up window or box. Always read the window or box to identify the program request and write down any confusing details. You can then contact a computer professional with this information and get it explained. Ignoring the box is unhealthy for your computer. If the information is clear, do the update.

"THERE IS NO PROGRAMING
LANGUAGE NO MATTER HOW
STRUCTURED THAT WILL PREVENT
PROGRAMMERS FROM MAKING BAD
PROGRAMS"

Larry Flon (1975)
"On research in structured programming"

9. WHICH PROGRAMS?

In this chapter, I want to list for you the programs that you should always update. These are always safe if you do them from the program's website. Some will do a good job from the pop-up box. It is always a good idea to keep programs updated.

1. Operating System (Windows®, MAC®)

2. Microsoft Office® Products

3. Adobe® Products

4. ITunes®

5. Skype® and other video chat programs

6. Anti-Malware

7. Browser Products, Firefox®, Opera®, Safari®

8. Browser Add-ons like Java®

9. Printer and scanner drivers

Other than the operating system, programs will require you to click on the pop-up box or link within the program.

The anti-malware program Avast® has a software updater component to notify you of software updates for many installed programs. If you use Avast® to protect your computer, you can use the software updater to keep an eye on the software updates for you. It will not do them automatically. The updater has buttons to go get the correct update.

A word of caution … malware writers know that certain programs are commonly updated. They use that information to trick you into clicking on a pop-up that says "your program needs updating, click here to update." Be careful with pop-up windows.

Programs that I know use a pop-up window for an update are:

Skype®, ITunes®, Adobe Air®

Most other software has a button or notification within the program and that will show when you run it.

Learn to read every window that appears when you are using the software that is installed. If you do not recognize the software name, it may be something that you did not purposely install. In that case, write it down and Google it before you install an update.

When you check Google, be aware that there are websites that will call all types of programs a virus. Look for the result where the website name matches the software or is from a known source such as Malwarebytes®.

Typing "is *software name* safe" in a search bar on Google will give you the information you need to make a good decision.

"A COMPUTER WILL DO WHAT YOU ASK IT TO DO, BUT THAT MAY BE VERY DIFFERENT FROM WHAT YOU HAD IN MIND."

-Joseph Weizenbaum

10. BEWARE THE ADD-ONS

Certain programs, usually free ones, during the update process, will offer an add-on program. Adobe programs do this.

When you start the update, about the second or third screen, there is a three-section box; the middle one offers the other program. Uncheck the boxes before you move to the next step.

It is not the end of the world if you move quickly through the update process and suddenly realize you have something installed you do not want. You can use Windows® program and features uninstaller to remove it. This is in the Control Panel section in Windows®.

This program uninstaller process may be something you are not familiar with, and many people when they see that area for the first time, see all kinds of programs that "they never use" and uninstall them. I suggest you do not do that without the advice of the computer tech.

Uninstalling some programs, without knowing why

they are there, can cause other programs to stop working correctly. I will be covering this subject in detail in a future book on computer cleaning.

I always advise to go slowly and deliberately through the update process for any program. You learn what the update is doing, identifying the process and familiarizing yourself with your computer. The more you know, the better.

"EDUCATION IS THE MOST POWERFUL WEAPON WHICH YOU CAN USE TO CHANGE THE WORLD"

-Nelson Mandela

11. PROGRAMS I USE AND APPRECIATE (For Free)

1. Anti-Malware - Avast®

I use this free program to protect my computer from infection. It has been free for years. The only requirement to use this program is to register it with your email address once a year. They do not SPAM, and my address has never been used, to my knowledge, for any other purpose.

Installation includes some components I do not use. I always chose custom installation, so that I can uncheck the components I do not use.

The paid version has some extras that are good for those that want complete Internet protection without having to do any of the work.

2. System Cleanup - Wise Disk Cleaner® and Wise Registry Cleaner®

I use the disk cleaner program to clean up Windows® temporary files, printer files, and junk from the Internet. These files build up every time the computer is used and cause it to run slower than it would if they were regularly removed.

The Wise Disk Cleaner® clears out junk from the computer in an efficient manner. But, if your system is damaged due to a computer infection, this cleaning can have an adverse effect. I have seen it change the icons that work from the task bar at the bottom of the screen. There is no solve for this except to reinstall Windows® from scratch. The missing taskbar icons can be removed and re-set on the taskbar. This process requires that you locate the program in file explorer, and right click on it to "add to taskbar".

The problem is not within Wise, but in the corruption of the Windows® system.

The registry is the part of the computer that works in the background when the Windows® operating system starts. Wise Registry Cleaner® is a product that keeps this area of the system running smoothly. It is designed to mark all unused registry items and suggest cleaning. I run Wise Registry Cleaner® about once every 3 months and after I uninstall a program.

3. Malware Scan - Malwarebytes®

A computer should be scanned for Malware infection monthly. Malware is short for malicious software. I have seen very few computers that have no malware on them. It is rare. There are levels of infectious Malware, starting with Adware. I go into this in detail on my website Malwaretruth.com. I have plans to do a book in this series on malware cleanup as well.

Malware causes computers to run poorly and often allows more complex infections to take hold.

Malwarebytes® offers a free version and a paid version. The paid version runs automatically to protect your computer and can be scheduled to scan.

4. Browser - Chrome

Chrome opens a separate instance of Internet browsing for each place you go. This means your banking and your email are not in the same Internet computer space. It prevents security breaches which is helpful for shopping and banking online.

Because of the way Chrome runs, it uses more memory. This means your computer could run slower with Chrome than it does with another browser.

I run Windows® 10 on my computers and it comes with a browser Microsoft® calls Edge. Microsoft® is not using Internet Explorer with Windows 10®. Edge has a completely different look than previous browsers. It may take some getting used to at first.

5. Non-Tracking Browser – Epic

I use Epic since introduced to it by a colleague. Epic does not send tracking data to any Internet source. Your surfing is completely private. Tracking data is what creates advertisements to appear that are directly associated with places you have surfed and items you have searched for on the Internet.

6. Free Office - Open Office®

Open Office® is a free version writing, spreadsheet and presentation program. The files can be saved to Microsoft Office® format and shared with others that run Word®, Excel® and PowerPoint®. It also opens those files created in the Microsoft® programs and allows you to edit them.

The top menu is visually similar for accessing the formatting and printing shortcuts.

Open Office® behaves and functions like Microsoft Office®. It creates documents that Microsoft Office® users can open, but requires you to set up the section for saving them automatically in the Microsoft format. By default, the documents are saved in Open Office format.

Important Note:

Free products require that you pay attention during the installation. Often you will notice a screen that offers additional software. You can opt-out by unchecking the agreement box. It may say, "I Decline". That opts you out of the extras, but continues to install the program.

Free programs may also stop being supported. Free programs are often created by a community of contributors. In this way, if the supporting community stops, the program may not be updated.

If you want to research other categories of free programs, use Google®. A search in Google® like this will show you many programs you didn't know were free; "Free software for _____."

"IN THE PAST IT NEVER OCCURRED TO ME THAT EVERY CASUAL REMARK OF MINE WOULD BE SNATCHED UP AND RECORDED. OTHERWISE I WOULD HAVE CREPT FURTHER INTO MY SHELL."

-Albert Einstein: The Human Side (1979)

12. FINAL THOUGHTS

Computers should be fun. They can stay fun if the maintenance is kept up. Running updates is one way to keep it fun.

It is my hope that you found the information in this book helpful. It is my desire that you can now view Windows® updates not as a necessary evil, but as an improvement for your system.

Should your computer misbehave after an update, contact a computer technician to help to figure out what went wrong. The sooner you do, the better the results. If you want to fix it yourself, try uninstalling the update before any other fix.

I invite your feedback. If you email me, add, in the subject line, I read your book. Then I will know I am speaking to one of my readers.

ABOUT THE AUTHOR

Circe Denyer has almost 30 years of experience in the computer technical field, specializing in computer infections and data loss. Semi-retired from that, she is a writer, photographer, book formatter and dabbler in graphic arts.

She designs for the online T-shirt store Neateeshirts, located at http://neateeshirts.com and Neateestuff on Zazzle at http://www.zazzle.com/neateestuff

Her photography is currently for sale on Dreamstime®, Twenty20® and Pixabay® online.

Her books are available online on Amazon®.

Her motto; "if it is not fun, I am not interested."

Website: http://circed.com Email: circe@circed.com

www.ingramcontent.com/pod-product-compliance
Lightning Source LLC
Chambersburg PA
CBHW070901070326
40690CB00009B/1938